Walks

Keswick
& the Northern Lakes

Walks Keswick
26 WALKS
2-10 mls (3-16km)

Graded
Short Strolls to
Long Hikes

HALLEWELL
Pocket Walking Guide

About This Book

The purpose of this book is to bring together under one cover, as compactly as possible, the bulk of the best walks around the town of Keswick plus a selection of the better routes in the surrounding hills and dales of the northern Lake District. These walks range from under a mile (1.5km) in length to 10 miles (16km); from testing hill climbs to the lightest of strolls.

● **Maps and Grades:** The centre pages provide a general map of the area, showing the whereabouts of each route, and a list of the contents. Each route is graded for difficulty: from **A+** for the most strenuous and difficult routes to **C** for the simplest low-level walks. A sketch map is provided for each route, but on **A** and **A+** graded walks the use of the relevant Ordnance Survey map is strongly recommended – both for personal safety and to enhance the enjoyment of the walks. Sheet numbers are shown above each route map (for both 1:50,000 and 1:25,000 series) and grid references are provided for the starts of the routes.

● **Safety:** The image of the Lakeland hills may be friendly, but their good nature should not be depended upon. In addition to maps, walkers on **A** and **A+** grade routes should take a compass (and know how to use it), suitable footwear, warm clothing, a small supply of food and drink and a full set of waterproofs. The weather can change very quickly, and the summits are generally much colder than the surrounding dales. In addition, anyone venturing into the hills should leave a note of their intended route with a third party. Most walkers encounter few serious difficulties, but there is no point in taking unnecessary risks.

This book cannot hope to be comprehensive – the Lake District has an extraordinary density of fine, varied walks – but it should serve as an introduction to one of the outstanding walking areas in the British Isles.

Key

═══ — *metalled Road*	Ⓟ — *parking*
┄┄┄ — *track*	(267 236) — *OS grid reference*
●●● — *route*	wc — *toilets*
◄ — *illustrated viewpoint*	200m — *contour: shaded area is above height indicated*

The Area

The shape of the landscape and the long-accepted routes of lines of communication crudely divide the Lake District into four distinct areas: east, south, west and north. This book covers the last of these: the town of Keswick, the dales which radiate from it and the hills which surround them. The area is flanked to the east by a high ridge comprised of Helvellyn and a string of lesser peaks; to the south by the mass of hills around Langdale, Borrowdale and Ennerdale.

At the heart of the area is Keswick: a neat, slate-built town by the northern end of Derwent Water; originally developed as a centre for mining but now the principal tourist and service centre for the northern Lakes. Keswick owes its success to its comparative accessibility, with the valley of the River Greta providing a conduit for the A66 to the east, and that of the River Derwent providing access from the north-west. The railway no longer passes through Keswick, but the bed of the old line through the Greta's narrow, wooded dale remains (*Walk 5*). To the south-east, the A591 climbs over the low northern ridge of Castlerigg Fell to pass down the eastern side of Thirlmere (*8*) before climbing to the watershed at Dunmail Rise and dropping beyond to Grasmere and Windermere (see *Walks Grasmere, Ambleside & Windermere*).

North of Keswick, in the V of the Derwent and the Greta, is the isolated knot of the northern fells. The two principal hills are Skiddaw (*1*) and Blencathra; their two peaks, rising steeply from the low ground to the south of the range, clearly visible from most high points in the area. Between the two is the narrow valley of the Glenderaterra Beck, overlooked to the west by the steep Lonscale Crags (*2*), while between Skiddaw and Keswick is the low hill of Latrigg (*3*): easily accessible from the town and providing splendid views across Derwent Water.

The lake – broad and irregularly shaped, and with a cluster of wooded islands at its northern end – can be explored from the water, using one of the ferries which regularly make a circuit of the landing stages around the shoreline. For those on foot, a number of short tours from Keswick are possible. The shortest are the brief walks to the fine viewpoints of Friar's Crag (*7*) and Castlehead (*6*). On the eastern side, a longer tour can be

(Continued inside back cover)

1 Skiddaw ———————————— A+

*A straight hill climb over clear ground, leading to tremendous views. The paths on this section are steep in places, but not difficult. The alternative return route is much steeper; dropping down to Millbeck from where there is a 2 mile/3km walk to the start by the public road. Length: **8 miles/13km** (circuit); Height Climbed: **2000ft/610m** (car park to summit), **600ft/180m** (Millbeck to car park).*

O.S. Sheet 89 (4)

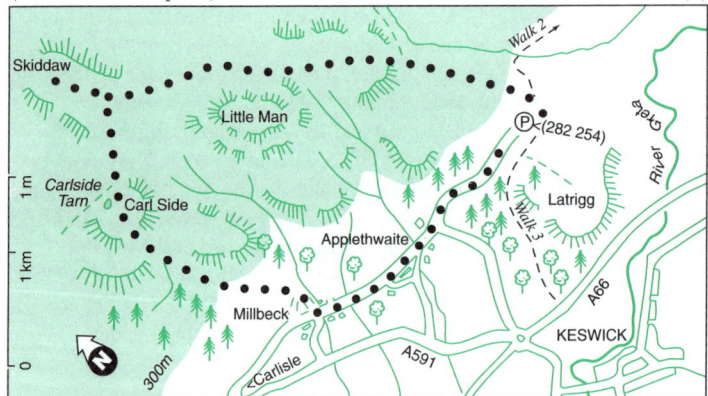

It is possible to reach the car park at the start of this route on foot from Keswick (see Walk 3). If you are travelling by car, drive north from Keswick on the A591 road for Carlisle. After passing the roundabout on the edge of the town, take the first road to the right. Follow this up to the foot of the hill and watch for a road cutting back to the right, signposted for Skiddaw. Turn on to this and follow it to the car park at its end.

The route to the summit presents few navigational difficulties. Walk out of the back of the car park and turn left along the signposted path. The path up the first climb – to the top of Little Man – is clearly visible; the route from there to the summit ridge is equally clear.

The easiest return is by the same route. For those who wish an alternative, however, there is a slightly longer and steeper return via Millbeck. For this, return to the southern end of the summit ridge and turn right, following a path which is faint at first, but which becomes clearer as it descends a steep, slippery scree slope (decent boots required). By the little tarn on the col at the foot of this slope there is a junction. For this route, carry straight on: over the low peak of Carl Side and down the shoulder of the hill beyond; dropping down to join the public road at the village of Millbeck. Turn left, and keep left at subsequent road junctions, to return to the start.

2 **Lonscale Crags** _____ **B**

A moderately long circuit across open country on the steep flanks of Skiddaw and Blencathra. Tracks generally clear, though rough and damp in places. Length: **7 miles/11km**; *Height Climbed:* **350ft/100m** *(from car park to the top of the walk),* **500ft/150m** *(Brundholme to car park).*

O. S. Sheets 89 or 90 (4)

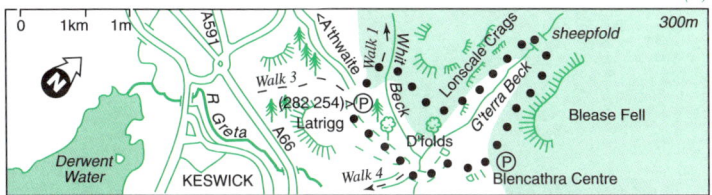

The start of this route can be reached on foot from Keswick – a distance of 2 miles/3km (one way) (see Walk 3). To reach it by car, drive north from the town on the A591 road for Carlisle. After passing the roundabout on the edge of the town turn first right, then first right again at the sign for Skiddaw, and follow the minor road to the car park at its conclusion.

Start the route as if climbing Skiddaw: walking out of the back of the car park and turning left. When the track splits after the second gate, however, go right; following a clear track which crosses Whit Beck and contours around the shoulder of Lonscale Fell before swinging left to run along the face of the Crags.

Continue on this track until a dyke heads off to the right, by an old sheepfold. Turn right at this point, dropping down to a footbridge over the beck and then swinging right down the far side of the valley. Follow this clear track to the car park at the Blencathra Centre. At the far end of the car park turn right through a gate and follow the

yellow arrows through the buildings. At the end of the buildings there is a junction of footpaths. Go right, in the direction signposted for Keswick, and follow the route marked by yellow arrows down to the public road. Turn right along this to reach the row of white cottages at Derwentfolds.

Look for the sign for the path to Keswick and go down the side of the buildings, following a sunken track down into the deep, wooded valley of the Glenderaterra Beck. Climb up beyond to the metalled road and turn right, continuing until a junction is reached. Turn left and, almost immediately, a track signposted for Skiddaw cuts off to the right.

At this point there is a choice. If you wish to walk back to Keswick by the River Greta, follow the return directions for Walk 4 (it is approx. 2 1/2 miles/4km to the centre of the town). To return to the car park, however, turn right. The track splits almost immediately. Stick to the clearer, right-hand track; climbing the buttress of Latrigg back to the car park.

3 Latrigg

A short circuit around a low, open hilltop, offering fine views over Derwent Water. Paths generally clear. Length: 2½ miles/4km; Height Climbed: 200ft/60m. If starting from Keswick, add: Length: 2 miles/3km (one way); Height Climbed: 650ft/200m.

O.S. Sheets 89 or 90 (4)

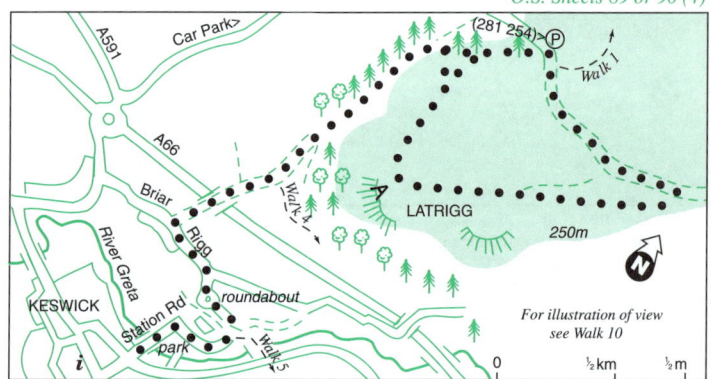

For illustration of view see Walk 10

This short walk can be started either from the car park at the beginning of the Skiddaw climb (see Walk 1) or from Keswick. From the car park, walk back to the entrance and turn left onto the start of the footpath signposted for Keswick. Rather than following the clear track by the side of the wood, however, contour around the round, open, grassy dome of the hill to reach the track leading to its low summit.

If you are starting from Keswick, walk north-east from the town centre on Station St, then continue along Station Rd across the River Greta. At the junction keep right, with Fitz Park to the right, and follow the road as it swings left under the old railway bridge and then continues to a small roundabout. Head right, then left at the next junction along Briar Rigg. Watch for the start of

the public bridleway, to the right of the road, signposted for Skiddaw.

Turn on to this clear track and follow it across the bridge over the A66 and on up the slope beyond, passing through farmland and mixed woodland. A short distance before the car park is reached (at the top of the wood), a grassy path cuts back to the right and climbs up to the summit of Latrigg.

From the summit, continue along a clear path leading down to a stile over a dyke. Continue straight ahead beyond this to a second field boundary. Here, turn left; down to a gate leading onto a clear track. A turn to the right at this point will link up with Walks 4 and 5, providing alternative returns to Keswick. For this route, however, turn left and follow the clear track back to the car park.

A signposted circuit to the north-east of Keswick; leading out and back through the mixed woodland on the steep slopes above the River Greta. Tracks generally clear. Length: (from centre of Keswick) **6 miles/9.5km**_; Height Climbed: undulating._

O.S. Sheets 89 or 90 (4)

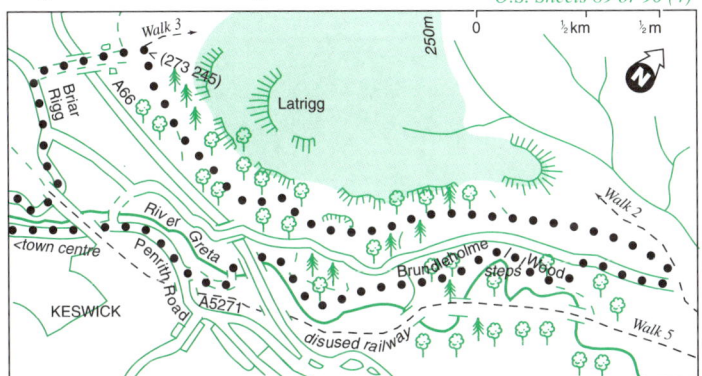

From Keswick, start this route as if walking to Latrigg (see Walk 3). After turning off Briar Rigg, follow the clear track across the A66 and up beyond until there is a sign to the right for the Brundholme Woods Circular Walk. Turn onto this path.

The path – through mixed woodland, including some fine oakwood – is crossed at a number of points by tracks and footpaths, but the route is marked at significant junctions by green arrows. After around one and a half miles (2.5km) the path emerges from the woods into an open area dotted with gorse, and drops gently along the eastern buttress of Latrigg to end at a stile leading onto the public road.

Turn right along this and continue until, just after an area of woodland begins to the left of the road, a footpath cuts off to the left signposted for Keswick. The path slants down through the wood to the side of the River Greta. A short detour to the left at this point would lead to a link with the old railway walk (visible on the far side of the river – see Walk 5). For this route, however, turn right, climbing a flight of steps above a bow in the river to reach a junction of paths. Keep left (signposted for Keswick). At the next three-way junction, keep straight on (once again signposted for Keswick).

The path eventually drops back down to the river and passes under the high bridge of the A66. A short way beyond this there is an old stone bridge crossing the river to the left. Walk across this and turn right to reach the A5271 (Penrith Road). Turn right again to return to the centre of Keswick.

5 Castlerigg Stone Circle ————————————— B

*A low-level route following the old railway line by the River Greta to the stone circle at Castlerigg, then returning to Keswick through farmland and woodland. The first section is clear; the return requires some navigation. Length: Up to **7 miles/11km**; Height Climbed: **400ft/120m** (undulating).*

O.S. Sheets 89 or 90 (4)

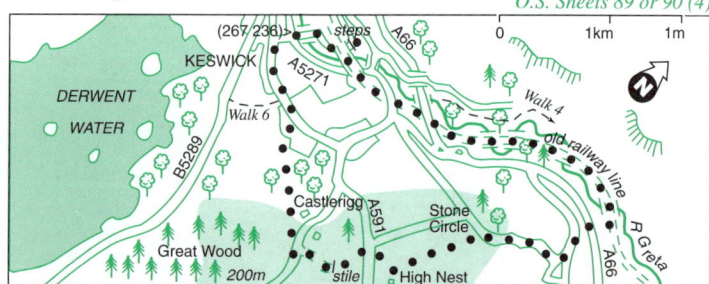

From the centre of Keswick, start this route as if climbing Latrigg (see Walk 3), but immediately after passing under the railway bridge turn right, climbing a flight of steps onto the old line. Turn left along this; following it out of the town, under the A66, and on along the wooded valley of the River Greta beyond.

Note from the map that there are three places where it is possible to cut left and return along the north side of the valley (see Walk 4); for this route, however, continue until, shortly after the line crosses the fourth bridge over the river, a signposted path for Castlerigg Stone Circle starts to the right. Follow this up a field to the A66. Cross the road – taking great care – and climb the slope beyond to reach a minor road. Turn left along this, then right at the next two junctions, to reach the stone circle.

Just before the field containing the circle is reached, a footpath cuts off to the left signposted for The Nest. Turn

onto this and follow a faint, grassy path through three fields, with a stile over each field boundary. At the end of the third field cross a stile and continue with a new plantation of trees to the left. Continue, now with a fence to the left, down to the barn at High Nest. Pass to the left of this, then to the right of a line of cottages, and follow the driveway beyond down to the A591.

Turn right along this, then cross over (carefully) opposite the junction with a narrow public road, and turn onto a public footpath signposted for Walla Crag. Walk up the right-hand side of the next three fields. After crossing the stile to leave the third of these fields, turn right onto a clear path, with a dyke to the right, which leads down to the public road. Turn left for a short distance, then right at the sign for a public footpath to Keswick. The return to Keswick from this point is as described in Walk 7.

6 Castlehead Wood _____ C

A short, low-level walk passing through two small woods on the edge of Keswick, providing excellent views of Derwent Water and the surrounding hills. Length: **2 miles/3km** *(from the centre of Keswick); Height Climbed:* **250ft/70m** *(if Castlehead is climbed).*

O.S. Sheets 89 or 90 (4)

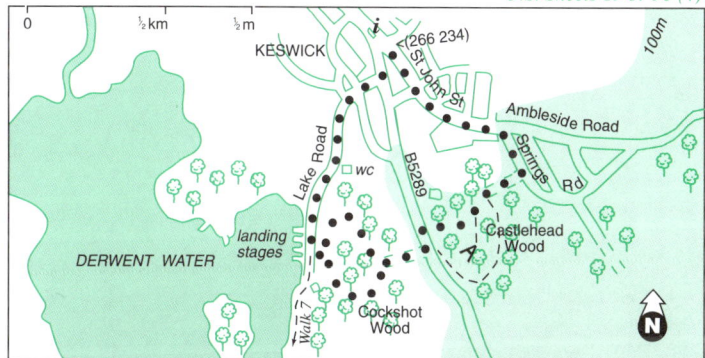

Starting from the tourist information centre in the centre of Keswick, walk south along St John's Street (becoming Ambleside Road). Follow this for around half a mile (1km) until Springs Road cuts off to the right. Turn down this and watch for the sign to the right for the public footpath to Castlehead. This marks the start of a metalled track which leads between two fields to a wooded hill, directly ahead.

There are clear tracks down either side of the wood. There is little difference between them in distance, but the right-hand path gives access to the short, steep path leading to the summit, from where there are excellent views.

Walk along the edge of the wood above the B5289 until the start of the track opposite becomes visible, then cross the road (carefully) and follow the clear track to Cockshott Wood, visible ahead. Once again there are paths down either side of the wood; both leading round the low hill to join Lake Road just by the landing stages.

1 Scafell Pike (978m) **2** Maiden Moor (576m) **3** Cat Bells (451m) **4** Rampsholme Island **5** Lord's Island **6** St Herbert's Island **7** Robinson (737m) **8** High Snockrigg (526m) **9** Derwent Island **10** Causey Pike (637m) **11** Crag Hill (839m) **12** Barrow (455m) **13** Grisedale Pike (791m)

7 Derwent Water and Walla Crag _____ B

*A moderately long circuit, starting through the woods by the lakeside, then climbing to return over the high crags. Tremendous views of Keswick, the lake and the surrounding hills. Length: up to **6 miles/9.5km**; Height Climbed: **950ft/290m**. This route can also be started from the car parks at Great Wood or Ashness Bridge, or by ferry from Keswick (see map).*

O.S. Sheets 89 or 90 (4)

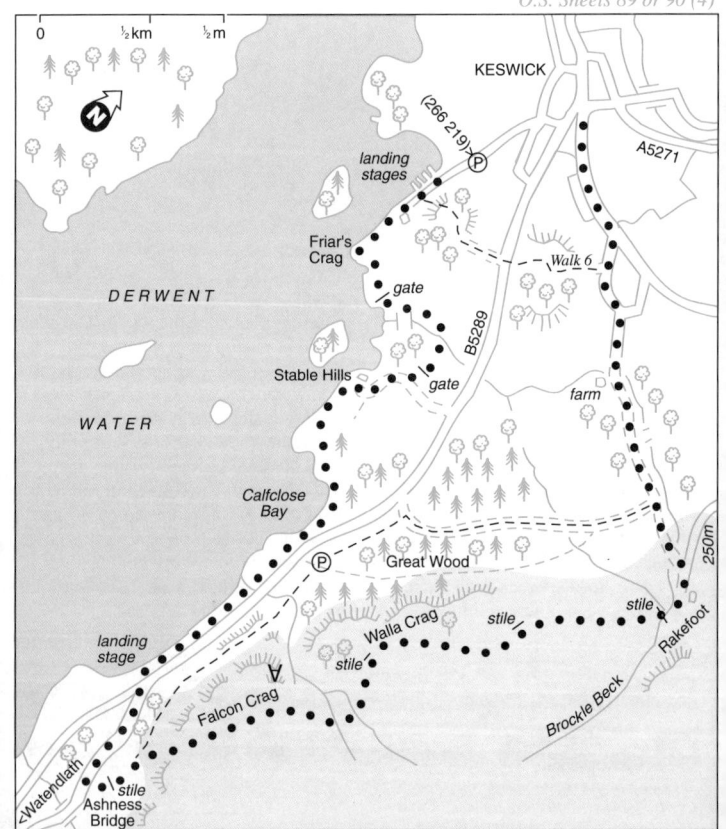

Start from the car park at Lake Road, in Keswick. Walk past the landing stages and on through the splendid woodland beyond to Friar's Crag. Double back from the rocky promontory and swing right through a grassy area behind the bay beyond. At the end of the bay go through a gate and continue with dense woodland to the right. This path crosses a footbridge over a small beck and then swings to the right, still with the wood to the right. Follow this track through a gate and up to a metalled road and then turn right, passing to the left of the house at Stable Hills. When a path cuts right, to the cottage, continue across a low rise and down to the lakeside beyond.

Follow the shore path round Calfclose Bay. When the B5289 comes in from the left, continue either over the rough ground by the lake or along the path by the road. (From the car park above the road at this point it is possible to make a shorter circuit back to Keswick: see map). Continue until the minor road for Watendlath leads up the hill to the left (if you are walking along the shore, this is just above the ferry landing stage). Turn up this and follow it until, just before the Ashness Bridge is reached, a clear path cuts off to the left,

heading towards a stile over a dyke. Beyond this the path splits, with one path running across the face of the hill and the other climbing up towards the rocky crags on the horizon. Take this latter path, up to and along the top of the crags and then down to join a dyke with a wood beyond it. There are stiles leading over the dyke to the viewpoints on Walla Crag beyond, but for this route continue with the dyke to the left.

Beyond the end of the wood the path drops down, with Brockle Beck to the right, to a dyke crossing the way. Cross a stile over this and then continue down with a dyke to the left. Swing right on a footbridge over the beck, then left, down the public road, with Rakefoot Farm to the right. After a short distance, cut left onto the signposted footpath for Keswick; dropping down to recross the burn, then climbing up to continue down the side of the wooded valley. At one point a clear track cuts off to the left for the Great Wood car park; otherwise, continue by the valley. A short distance beyond the junction the path drops down to a bridge over the beck. Ignore this and continue down the near side, passing through a group of farm buildings to join the public road. Carry straight on to return to Keswick.

1 *Grisedale Pike (791m)* 2 *St Herbert's Island* 3 *Swinside (244m)* 4 *Braithwaite* 5 *Rampsholme Island*
6 *Portinscale* 7 *Bassenthwaite Lake* 8 *Derwent Island* 9 *Lord's Island* 10 *Skiddaw (931m)* 11 *Latrigg (367m)*
12 *Walla Crag*

A varied circuit to the east of Thirlmere, passing through mixed woodland by the lakeside and returning along the open hillside above the fields overlooking the lake. Paths rough in places but generally clear. Length: **5 miles/8km***; Height Climbed:* **400ft/120m***.*

O.S. Sheet 90 (4 or 5)

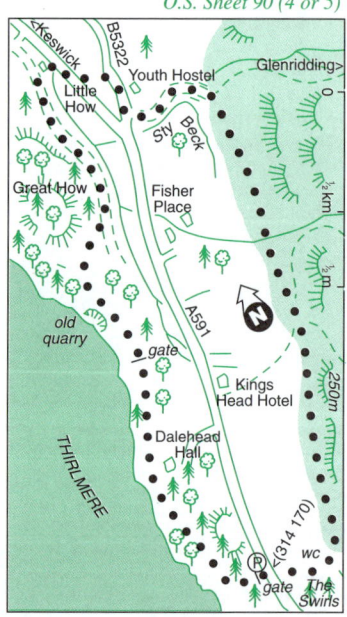

To reach the start of this route, drive south from Keswick on the A591. After six miles the road passes the Kings Head Hotel, overlooking Thirlmere. About a mile beyond this there are car parks to the left and right of the road.

Start the walk from the side of the road above the lake. Go through a gate marked by a signpost for the path to Great How and then follow the path, well marked by white arrows, down to the lakeside. This then turns to the right, through the woodland above the shore. There are numerous small paths through the trees but the route is in little doubt. At one point it crosses an open area in front of Dalehead Hall. Carry straight on across this and into the woods beyond. A little further on, after going through a gate, it appears to split. Keep to the right, above an old quarry by the waterside, and follow the clear path to the edge of Great How. Tracks go to left and right around the hill. For this route go right; dropping down to join a clear track and turning left along this to reach the main road by the buildings at Little How.

Cross the road at this point (taking great care) and turn right. After a short distance a signposted footpath starts to the left, leading up the right-hand side of a field to join the B5322. Turn right along this for a short distance, then turn left at a junction, just beyond the Youth Hostel, on a road signposted as a bridleway to Glenridding. Follow this

up the left-hand side of the Sty Beck. Above the top dyke there is a bridge to the right, just below a fall in the beck. Cross this and carry on along a clear path. After a short distance turn off the Glenridding track onto a path signposted for Swirls car park. Follow this rough footpath along the open slope above a dyke to a junction of footpaths on the edge of a conifer plantation. Turn right at this point to return to the car park.

A long, steady hill climb providing splendid views, with a return through craggy mountain scenery. Length: **8 miles/13km***; Height Climbed:* **2200ft/670m***. Paths clear but rough in places.*

O.S. Sheets 89 or 90 (4)

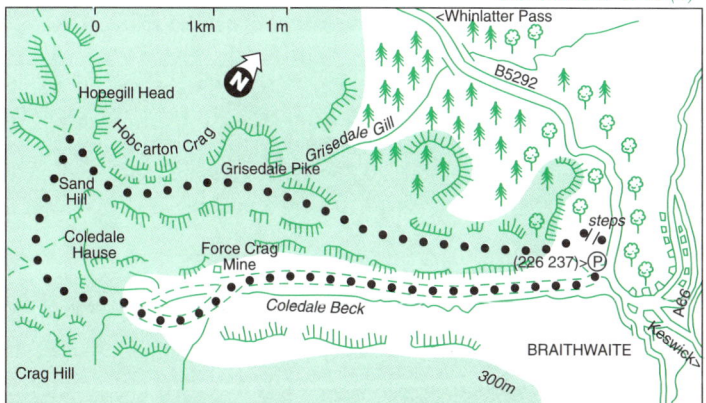

To reach the start of this route, drive west from Keswick on the A66 for Cockermouth. Two miles from the centre of Keswick the B5292 cuts off to the left into Braithwaite. Follow this road (signposted for the Whinlatter Pass) through the village and up the narrow valley beyond. A short distance beyond the village there is a small car park to the left of the road.

Two paths leave this car park. Take the path signposted for Grisedale Pike; climbing – on steps at first – onto the ridge above and then swinging left with trees down to the right. Follow this clear path up to the summit of Grisedale Pike, from where there are fine views of Skiddaw and Keswick.

For a shorter version of this walk, simply retrace your steps. To return by Coledale, carry straight on across the summit and continue along the rough path beyond, along the edge of Hobcarton Crag to the rocky peak of Hopegill Head. One path cuts off to the right at this point, while another continues along the ridge beyond (leading down to Crummock Water). For this route, however, turn left on a clear path dropping down to the col of Coledale Hause.

On the far side of the hause there is a junction, with one path dropping down towards Crummock Water to the right and another climbing the narrow dale ahead to reach the peaks of Grassmoor and Crag Hill. For this route, however, turn left; dropping steeply down by the headwaters of the Coledale Beck to join the clear track running up the dale to the old Force Crag mine. Turn down this and follow it back to the start.

A complicated but pleasant low-level circuit from Keswick; heading west to Portinscale, then south through the mixed woodland above Derwent Water, before returning by the valley of the Newlands Beck. Paths generally clear. Length: (from centre of Keswick) **8 miles/13km**; *Height Climbed: undulating.*

O.S. Sheets 89 or 90 (4)

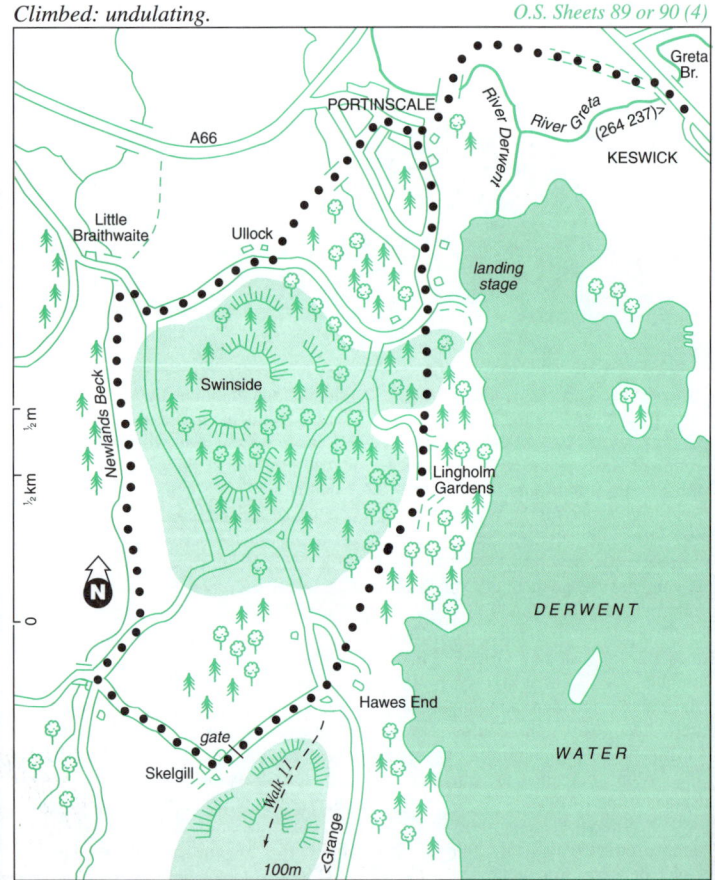

Walk west from the centre of Keswick on the main road. Immediately after crossing Greta Bridge turn onto a track which cuts off to the left, signposted for Portinscale. When the building ends to the right swing right and follow a clear path across the flood-plain to a bridge over the River Derwent. Cross this and walk straight ahead into the centre of the village of Portinscale.

At the road junction turn left, following the sign for Grange. Continue on this road until, just beyond the point where a public road cuts down to a landing stage to the left, there is a gap in the beech hedge to the left of the road. Go through this and bear right, climbing a low, wooded hill on a clear path. A little beyond the summit of the hill a track cuts off to the left. Ignore this and carry straight on to join the metalled road leading to Lingholm Gardens. Just to the right of the entrance to the gardens there is a pedestrian gate. Go through this and follow the clear path beyond which leads up to a junction above Hawes End.

Swing half-right up a rough path with a dyke to the right and a wooded hill to the left. This leads to a narrow public road. Follow this uphill to a further junction and continue along the road signposted for Skelgill. Go through the gate above Skelgill and continue along the narrow public road beyond; down through the buildings and on to a T-junction. Turn right and walk on until, at the point where the road and the beck begin to diverge, a public footpath cuts off to the left signposted for Portinscale.

The footpath follows the beckside for a mile (1.5km) until a minor road crosses the way at Little Braithwaite. Turn right along this road and follow it for about half a mile: keeping left at the junction and continuing until, just beyond the last building at Ullock Farm, a signposted footpath leads off to the left. The path starts between two fences; jinking to right and left at the end of the building to the left, then passing through a gate and continuing along the left-hand side of a field. The path is quite clear; passing through two fields before reaching a footbridge over a beck at the foot of a wooded slope. Cross the bridge and climb the path up the slope beyond to join a road. Turn left along this for a few steps, then right, through a gate and along the path beyond, to a junction with another road. Turn right along this to return to the centre of Portinscale, then left to return to Keswick along the original path.

1 *King's How (392m)* 2 *Glaramara (783m)* 3 *Great End (910m)* 4 *Scafell Pike (978m)* 5 *Dale Head (753m)*
6 *Cat Bells (451m)* 7 *Hindscarth (727m)* 8 *Robinson (737m)* 9 *High Stile (807m)* 10 *Causey Pike (637m)*
11 *Crag Hill (839m)* 12 *Coledale Hause* **(See Walk 3)**

11 **Cat Bells and Derwent Water** _____ A

A steep climb across open ground, leading to splendid views over Derwent Water and the surrounding hills, followed by an equally steep descent and a return through the woodland by the edge of the lake. Length: **6 miles/ 9.5km***; Height Climbed:* **1100ft/330m.** *Paths clear, but rough and damp in places. Possible alternative low-level route of similar distance (see map).*

O.S. Sheets 89 or 90 (4)

Map labels: Walk 10; <Keswick; gate; DERWENT WATER; landing stage; gate; Hawes End; (247 212) > P; low level alternative; Skelgill; landing stage; Brandelhow Bay; Abbot's Bay; Myrtle Bay; gate; Brandelhow; gate; bridges; Lodore >; CAT BELLS; gate; gate; N; gate; Grange >; 250m; High Spy >; Youdale Knot Farm; gate; 0 ½km ½m

The start of this route can be reached by following the early section of Walk 10: a distance of 2½ miles (4km), one way, from the centre of Keswick. By car, drive west from Keswick on the A66 and turn first left on the road for Portinscale. Drive through the village and on along the minor road signposted for Grange. After about two miles there is a multiple junction. Turn right onto the road signposted for Skelgill and park in the small car park on the left.

Walk back to the junction and turn up the clear path; climbing up to the ridge leading to the summit of Cat Bells. (For the alternative, low-level version of this route, follow the Grange road for a short distance then cut right onto a clear track, signposted as a bridleway). The views from this ridge are superb, and a clear track can be seen continuing beyond; climbing up to High Spy and Dale Head. For this route, however, drop down to the col beyond the summit and turn left onto a clear path which descends steeply to the road. (Note the end of the alternative route to the left at this point.)

Turn right along the road (narrow in places, and sometimes busy, so take great care). A short way after passing Youdale Knot Farm there is a gate to the left of the road and a sign for a footpath to Lodore. Follow this faint path across an open area to the right-hand corner of a wood surrounded by a dyke. Go through a kissing gate in a dyke to the right of this and continue with the wood to the left. At the next dyke there is a further gate and a split in the path. The right-hand path crosses the head of the lake to join the main road at Lodore. For this route, however, keep to the left: following a rough, grassy path which starts by running approximately parallel to the edge of the wood. As the path approaches the lake a further path cuts off to the right. Ignore this and carry on; crossing narrow wooden footbridges over an area of marsh and then continuing with the lake to the right.

Near the head of Myrtle Bay, pass through a gate in a well-maintained dyke and continue on a path through an area of splendid oak woodland. This soon joins the metalled driveway into Abbot's Bay. Turn right along this for a short distance until it splits, then keep left, around the head of the bay (following the signs for the footpath to Keswick) and up to the house at Brandelhow. Pass between the house and its garage and then continue around the head of the bay. Near the end of the bay a stile crosses the fence to the right. Ignore this and swing inland, uphill, until a gate appears in the dyke to the right. Go through this into an area of woodland criss-crossed by paths. Keep close to the lakeside. Almost immediately the path passes one of the ferry landing stages (a possible return route for a walk from Keswick: check times and prices locally).

A little over half a mile (1km) further on, through pleasant mixed woodland, a second landing stage is reached; this one at the point where a dyke with a kissing gate in it crosses the way. Pass through this, into a field, and swing left along a path – faint at first, but gradually becoming clearer – along the left-hand edge of the field. When a gate is reached to the left turn through it, passing through a narrow band of trees. On the far side of the trees swing right, following a clear track towards a house, visible ahead. Pass through a gate and continue along the clear track which passes in front of the house and continues up the field beyond. Pass through the gate at the top of the field and on to the metalled road beyond. Turn right along this (signposted for Keswick) and follow it up to the road. Turn left to return to the car park.

Walks Keswick & the Northern Lakes

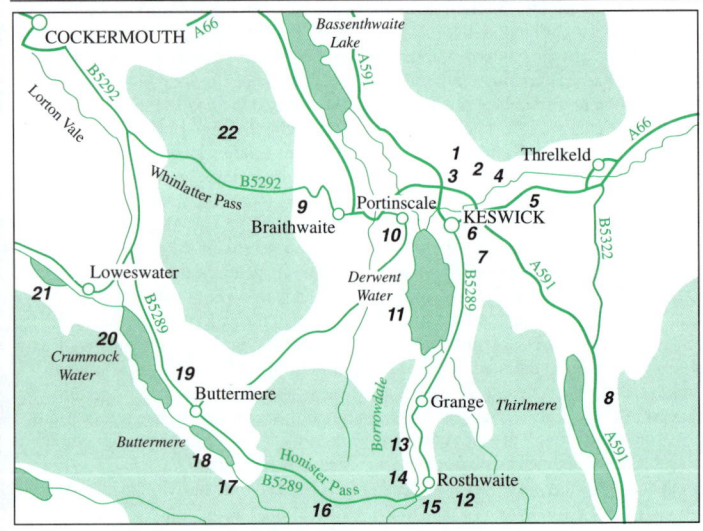

Local and topographic terms

Beck — Stream

Cairn — Pile of stones

Col — Low point between two peaks

Dale — Valley

Dyke — Dry-stone wall

Fell — Mountain

Force — Waterfall

Garth — Enclosure, farmyard

Gill, ghyll — Ravine, stream within it

Mere — Lake

Pike — Peak

Scale — Herdsman's hut

Steadings — Farm outbuildings

Syke — Small stream

Tarn — Small lake

Thwaite — Clearing for pasture

Published by: Hallewell Publications, Port-an-Eilean,
Strathtummel, Perthshire, PH16 5RU
Printed by Harley & Cox Ltd, Dundee.

Walks Keswick & the Northern Lakes

Grades

A+ .... Full walking equipment – including map and compass – and previous hill walking experience essential

A ...... Full walking equipment required

B ...... Strong footwear and waterproof clothing required

C ...... Comfortable footwear recommended

12 Rosthwaite, Watendlath and Stonethwaite —— A

A high circuit across open moorland, passing two fine tarns along the way. The paths are rough and damp in places, and the long, steep descent to Stonethwaite is, though scenically superb, tough on the knees. Length: **6 miles/9.5km**; *Height Climbed* **1100ft/340m.**

O.S. Sheets 89 or 90 (4)

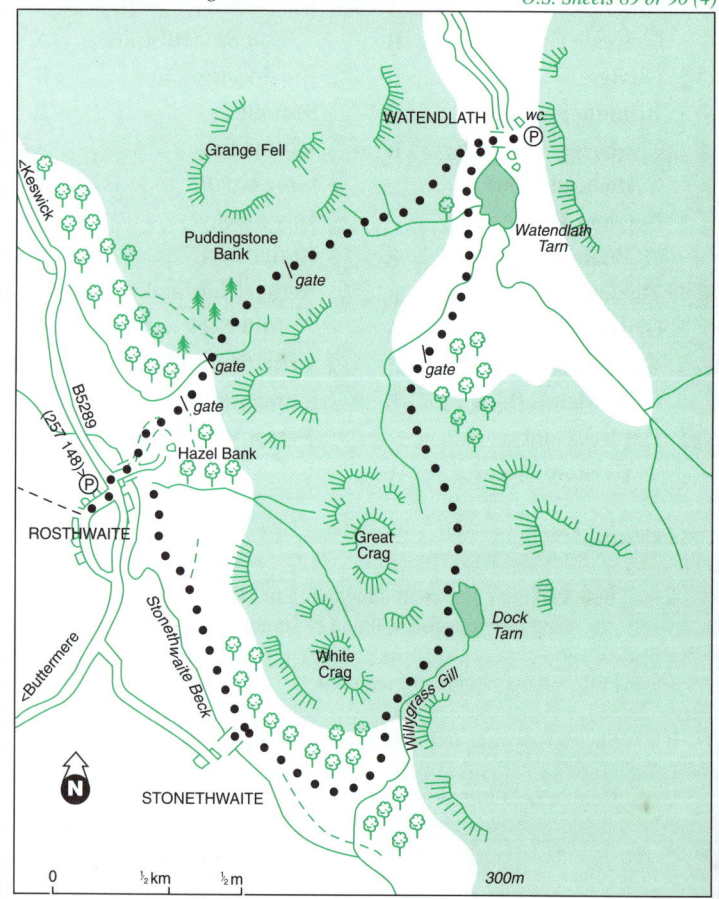

To reach Rosthwaite, drive six miles south of Keswick on the B5289 road for Borrowdale. Turn right in the village and park in the car park.

Walk back up to the main road and turn left. After a short distance turn first right at the sign for Hazel Bank. Cross the green slate bridge over Stonethwaite Beck and turn left at the junction beyond, following the signpost for the public footpath to Watendlath.

The route is clear: flat at first, between dykes, then swinging to the right and starting to climb the slope. After a short climb the path reaches a gate in a dyke running across the slope. Go through this and climb up to a further dyke. Pass through the gate in this, cross the footbridge over a small beck just beyond, then continue climbing to the right of a dyke. After a short distance there is a gate in this dyke and a sign for a footpath to Keswick. Ignore this and carry straight on: climbing up to the gate in the neck of the hill pass, passing through this and then dropping down the slope beyond, following the clear path leading to the pleasant cluster of buildings at Watendlath.

Double back from the hamlet on the same route; this time swinging left, by the side of the tarn, on the track signposted for Dock Tarn. After a short distance there are two gates ahead, side by side. Go through the right-hand gate and continue on a clear path between dykes.

At the end of this alleyway there is a gate with a stile beside it. Cross the stile and carry straight on, for a short distance, before crossing the small beck which crosses the way and then turning right to follow the path beside it. This leads up to a dyke. Turn left along this and follow it to another beck. Cross this and turn right (at this point there is a blue arrow to mark the route) and climb up the hill, with a dyke to the right, to a further dyke crossing the way. Go through the kissing gate in this dyke and turn left; following a rough but clear (waymarked) footpath over the open ground up to Dock Tarn.

Follow the path round the right-hand edge of this beautiful hill tarn, then continue beyond; swinging right and dropping down the path to the right of Willygrass Gill. This is a splendid section, but very steep; eventually becoming a stone staircase on the precipitous descent through the fine oak woods above the valley of the Stonethwaite Beck.

Follow the clear path down to the junction with the Cumbria Way. Turn right along this and follow it (making a brief diversion to visit the charming little village of Stonethwaite) back to Rosthwaite.

A short circuit on clear tracks and rough footpaths, passing through arable farmland and mixed woodland, and featuring a dramatic hill-pass and a pleasant section by the River Derwent. Length: **4 miles/ 6.5km**; *Height Climbed:* **350ft/100m.**

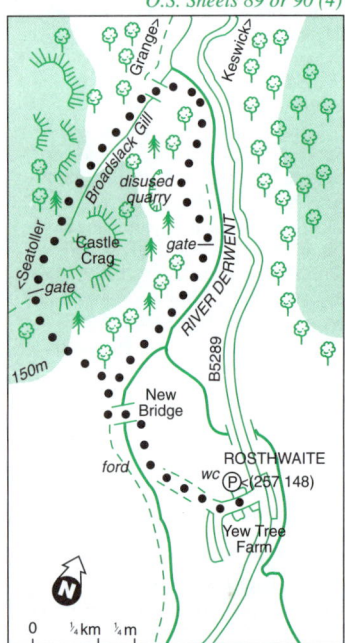

O.S. Sheets 89 or 90 (4)

To reach Rosthwaite, drive six miles south of Keswick on the B5289 road for Borrowdale. Turn right in the village to reach the car park and start walking down the road which continues beyond. Follow the direction indicated by the sign for the footpath to Grange: past Yew Tree Farm; through the steadings beyond; then on across an area of fields, with dykes to either side.

When the track reaches the river, swing to the right and follow it downstream to New Bridge. Cross this and turn right at the far end, continuing to walk by the river and ignoring tracks cutting off to the left until the main track reaches an area of mixed woodland. At this point it swings left itself. Follow it through a gate and into the wood proper. At one point there is a split. Keep to the left and follow the track up to the old slate quarries in the heart of the wood.

Just beyond the quarries the path goes through a narrow gap in a fine slate dyke and then continues; passing through another dyke and then swinging right, back down towards the river. Continue by the water until the point where Broadslack Gill flows into a wide pool at a bend in the river. Cross a small footbridge over the gill and then, rather than continuing by the river, turn left on a clear path, signposted for Seatoller, which climbs by the side of the stream.

Follow this splendid path out of the wood and into an open hill-pass with dramatic rocks and scree to either side. Just beyond the neck of the pass there is a gate in the dyke to the left. Go through this and follow the faint footpath beyond, dropping down through two fields to rejoin the original path a little downstream from the hump-backed New Bridge. Either cross here or continue to the stepping-stones at the ford upstream.

A short circuit on rough tracks and footpaths, through farmland and mixed woodland, featuring fine views of the hills around Borrowdale. Length: **3 miles/4.5km**; *Height Climbed:* **400ft/120m**.

O.S. Sheets 89 or 90 (4)

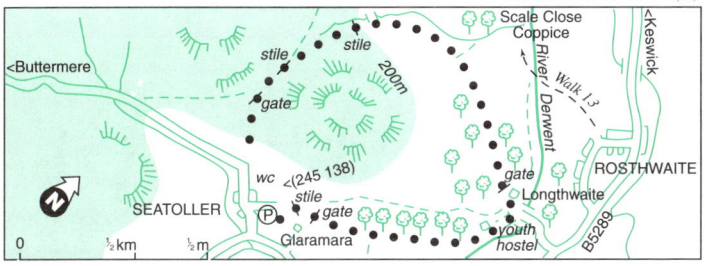

To reach Seatoller, drive seven miles south of Keswick on the B5289 road signposted for Borrowdale. Start walking from the car park on the edge of the little village; heading out of the back of the parking area along the path signposted for Longthwaite.

The track leads to a stile, then splits immediately beyond. Go right, with a dyke to the right, and continue to a gate behind the lodge at Glaramara. Beyond this a rough footpath continues through mixed woodland, with the flood plain, criss-crossed by dykes, down to the right. Half a mile (1km) from the start of the walk, the River Derwent converges with the steep wooded slope to the left, and the footpath has to scramble across a rocky outcrop before continuing past the Youth Hostel to the farm buildings at Longthwaite.

At this point there is a junction: to the right a bridge crosses the river, while a clear track carries straight on ahead. Take neither of these. Turn left instead, following a faint, grassy path up the near side of the buildings. Pass through

a gate at the back of the steadings and continue with a dyke to the right. A clear path leads along the face of the slope for a further half mile (1km) before exiting the woods.

To the right at this point is a wooded valley around a small beck. Follow the grassy path which heads across the slope towards the National Trust woodland at Scale Close Coppice. At the point where the path reaches the coppice it splits: take the left-hand path, swinging up towards a dyke crossed by a tall stile. Cross this and continue along a faint grassy path until a stile is visible over the dyke to the right. Walk over to this, cross it, and then turn left along a clear track beyond.

Follow this track down to a corner formed by two dykes in which there are two gates. Go through the left-hand gate and follow a path down to a junction of tracks. Carry straight on downhill for a short distance. When the main track swings left, take the clear path to the right; dropping down to join the public road just above Seatoller.

*A long, steep hill climb over rough ground, passing through splendid mountain scenery. Length: **10 miles/16km**; Height Climbed: **2250ft/682m** (undulating). The paths are generally rough and some navigation is required in places, but the summit views are superb.*

O.S. Sheets 89 or 90 (4)

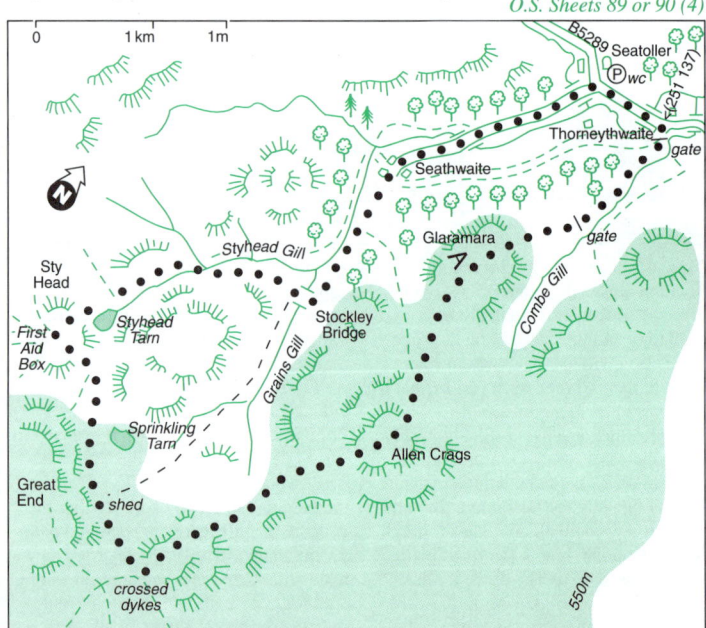

To reach the start of the route, drive south from Keswick on the B5289 road signposted for Borrowdale. Follow this for around seven miles until, just before it begins to climb up to the Honister Pass, it reaches the little village of Seatoller. Park in the car park on the edge of the village (if this is full, drive back a short way and turn right, up to

the car park at Seathwaite – also on the route).

From Seatoller, walk back along the road for half a mile (1km) to the road bridge over the River Derwent. Just beyond this, turn right onto the tarmac road signposted for Thorneythwaite. After a short distance there is a gate to the left of the road, beside which there is a stile and a sign for a public footpath. Turn left at this point and follow a clear path which climbs up to the corner of an area of broad-leaved woodland and then swings right, following the line of a dyke. The track remains clear at first, climbing gently along the left-hand edge of a ridge with the Combe Gill tumbling over its waterfall below. After passing through a gate in a dyke, however, the precise line of the path becomes less clear, though there is little difficulty with the route: climb gradually onto the top of the ridge to the right and then continue climbing to the rocky outcrops on the summit of Glaramara. Scramble up these and – weather allowing – enjoy the spectacular views of the surrounding peaks.

The next section requires more care, as it is easy to go wrong amongst the mass of peaks and ridges beyond the summit. To the south-west is the vast cliff-faced mass of Great End. Drop down onto the broad ridge which heads approximately towards it (the route is marked by cairns); skirting to the left of a second, lower summit; dropping down to a second col, peppered by small tarns; then climbing to the low summit of Allen Crags.

Drop down beyond this to a clear junction of paths, marked by two short dykes arranged in a cross. Turn right at this point and follow a path downhill by the side of a small stream, with the cliffs of Great End up to the left. At a small shed there is a junction, with one path peeling off to the right to follow Grains Gill down to Stockley Bridge (an alternative ending to this walk: see map). For this route, however, carry straight on; passing Sprinkling Tarn and then dropping down to a clear junction of paths at Sty Head (marked by a first-aid box). At this point, the track down into Wasdale heads off to the left, while the path up Great Gable climbs steeply up the ridge directly ahead.

For this walk turn right; following a clear path down the valley of Styhead Gill. A short distance after passing Styhead Tarn the path splits. Go right, crossing the footbridge over the gill and following an increasingly steep path; running beside a deep, wooded gully at first, then swinging right to drop down to the hump-backed Stockley Bridge. Cross this and turn left, along a clear track, down the dale to the farm at Seathwaite and to the public road beyond.

1 *Great End (910m)* 2 *Lingmell (800m)* 3 *Yewbarrow (610m)* 4 *Great Gable (899m)* 5 *Green Gable (801m)* 6 *Pillar (892m)* 7 *Brandreth (715m)* 8 *High Stile (807m)*

A high-level circuit on rough paths, faint in places, leading out across a splendid mountain plateau dotted by small tarns and returning via an old slaters' road. Wonderful views of the surrounding peaks. Length: **4miles/ 6.5km**; *Height Climbed:* **1200ft/355m**.

O.S. Sheets 89 or 90 (4)

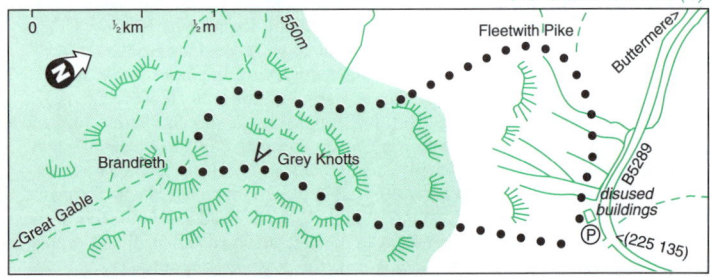

To reach the start of the route, drive 10 miles south of Keswick on the B5289 road to Buttermere; climbing up from Borrowdale into the neck of the Honister Pass. The car park is to the left of the road, shortly before the disused buildings of the slate-mining company.

There are signposts in the car park indicating two public footpaths. Look for the path to Grey Knotts, heading directly up the slope behind the car park. This is the less clear of the two paths and starts unpromisingly; climbing steeply up a damp slope to the left of a fence. Continue to the top of the hill: ignoring the first two stiles to the right, then taking the third in order to

reach the summit. The views from the top are superb.

Directly ahead is the pronounced mound of Great Gable, and a little to the right of that, nearer at hand, is the low, rounded top of Brandreth. Head towards the latter, walking across a splendid, broad-topped ridge. Beyond the summit, a path continues to Great Gable. For this route, however, turn right from the peak and follow a faint path which gradually swings back to the right to run parallel to the ridge above, before running down the north-western edge of Grey Knotts to join the old slaters' road in the shadow of Fleetwith Pike. Turn right along this to return to the car park.

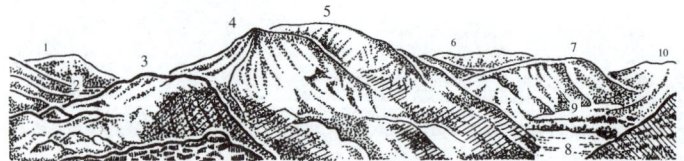

1 *Crag Fell (523m)* 2 *Ennerdale Water* 3 *Haystacks (597m)* 4 *High Crag (744m)* 5 *High Stile (807m)* 6 *Hen Comb (509m)* 7 *Mellbreak (512m)* 8 *Buttermere* 9 *Crummock Water* 10 *Loweswater Fell*

A gruelling but dramatic high-level circuit, passing across open moorland and along a section of a fine ridge. The route is clear, but very rough and steep in places. The views are matchless. Length: **6 miles/9.5km**; Height Climbed: **1650ft/500m**.

O.S. Sheets 89 or 90 (4)

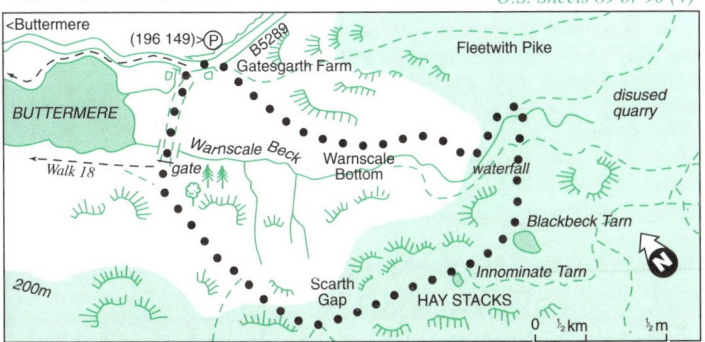

Park in the car park at Gatesgarth Farm, at the eastern end of Buttermere, and start walking along the public road, away from the lake. After a short distance there is a sign for a public bridleway to the right of the road. Turn onto this and follow the clear track which sets off to the right of the hill; swinging left into the flat valley floor of Warnscale Bottom, surrounded by majestic peaks and cliff faces.

There are two clear paths climbing the head of the valley. Either will do, but the one to the left of Warnscale Beck, climbing gradually across a scree slope dotted with dwarf trees, is the easier. Once at the top of the slope, just beyond the waterfall, a clear path heads off to the right. Turn on to this and follow it to the foot of Blackbeck Tarn. From here there is a truly spectacular view between massive rock outcrops, down to Buttermere and beyond.

Continue beyond, following the rough, winding footpath along the jagged ridge of Hay Stacks. A certain amount of scrambling will be required around the peak itself, at which point any path effectively disappears. Beyond the peak, however, it reappears; dropping down steeply into Scarth Gap. On the col there is a junction of tracks: the one to the left dropping down into Ennerdale, while another continues along the ridge above Buttermere. For this route, however, turn right; dropping steeply across scree towards the head of the lake. Near the bottom of the slope the path runs to the left of a wood. At the end of the wood there is a junction. Keep right at this point, with the wood still to the right, and follow the path down to a gate in a dyke. Cross Warnscale Beck beyond this and continue across the valley bottom back to Gatesgarth.

*A circuit of a small lake, surrounded by high, dramatic peaks. The
footpaths are rough in places but the route is easily followed. Length:*
4¹/₂ miles/7km; *Height Climbed: negligible.*

O.S. Sheets 89 or 90 (4)

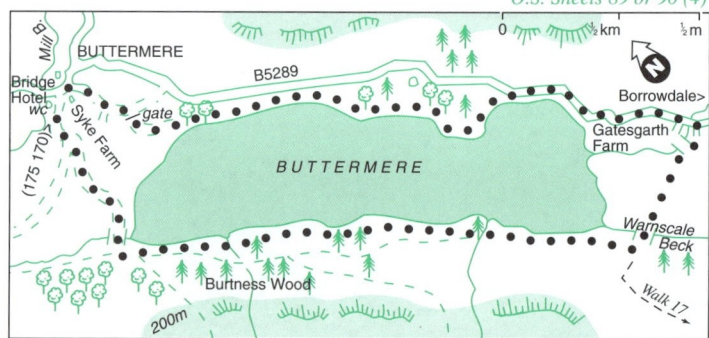

Park in one of the various car parks in
Buttermere village and look for the
Bridge Hotel by Mill Beck. On the far
side of the hotel from the beck there is a
signpost for the entrance to Syke Farm
and for a public bridleway leading to the
lake shore. Walk through the farm and
through the gate at the far end of the
buildings, and then continue along a
clear path beyond. At the next field
boundary there is a junction. Turn right
and follow a clearly signposted footpath
down to the water's edge.

Follow the permissive footpath (all
dogs to be kept under strict control)
through a fine area of woodland and
fields by the lakeside until the shore
swings round to converge with the
public road up to the left. Continue
along the side of the road until the
entrance to Gatesgarth Farm is reached,
shortly beyond the head of the lake.

Turn right through this and follow the
track signposted for Buttermere across
an area of flat farmland. On the far side
of the dale, just after crossing a bridge
over Warnscale Beck, there is a split in
the track: one clear path carrying
straight on up the steep slope ahead,
signposted for Scarth Gap (between Hay
Stacks *(17)* and High Crag) and
Ennerdale, and the other heading right,
back towards the lake. Turn right.

After half a mile (1km) there is a
split in the lakeside track. Keep to the
right at this point and follow the
permissive footpath through the trees by
the water's edge. At the foot of the lake
the track splits again. Go right, crossing
the beck and continuing on a clear track
across the flat isthmus between
Buttermere and Crummock Water, back
to Buttermere.

19 **Nether How and Mill Beck** _____ C

A short circuit through the farmland, mixed woodland and grazing land between Buttermere and Crummock Water, providing fine views of both lakes and of the surrounding hills. Length: **2 miles/3km**; *Height Climbed:* **250ft/80m**.

O.S. Sheets 89 (4)

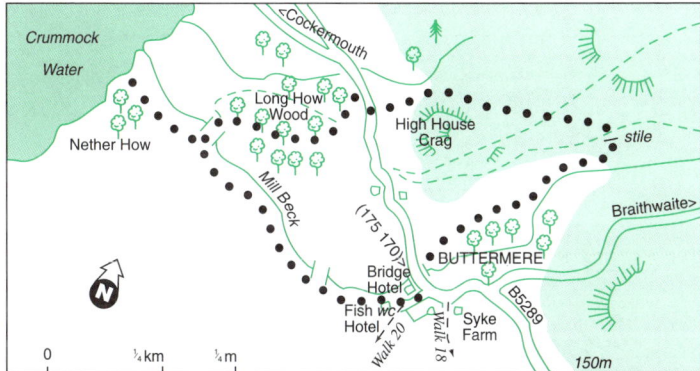

Park in one of the numerous car parks around Buttermere village and walk to the Bridge Hotel, just where the road runs over the Mill Beck. Turn down the road by the side of the hotel and then go to the right of the Fish Hotel (passing a further parking area). This road continues as a footpath to the left of the Mill Beck, skirting the alluvial isthmus between Buttermere and Crummock Water.

Follow the path down to the oak-covered mound of Nether How – visible ahead – at the end of Crummock Water. From here there are splendid views of the lake and the surrounding hills.

To continue, double back on the same path until a bridge crosses the beck to the left. Cross this and turn right, following a clear footpath up through Long How Wood to the public road. Turn right along this for a short distance, then cross the road (carefully) and go over the stile by the sign for a public footpath. The path climbs between a dyke and a steep slope, gradually swinging to the right and climbing onto a low col. There is a confusion of paths at this point. Cross the col – continuing in approximately the direction you were going before – and look for the area of woodland around the Mill Beck beyond. Drop down to the top of this wood and look for a stile over a dyke leading into the trees. Cross this and follow the clear path beyond; dropping down through this fine area of woodland, with the beck below and to the left, to rejoin the road opposite the Bridge Hotel.

*A moderately difficult circuit of Crummock Water on paths of varying quality – rough and wet in places; faint in others – passing through woodland and rough grazing land by the water's edge. Fine views of the surrounding hills. Length: **9 miles/14.5km**; Height Climbed: **650ft/200m** (on extension up Rannerdale; otherwise negligible).*

O.S. Sheet 89 (4)

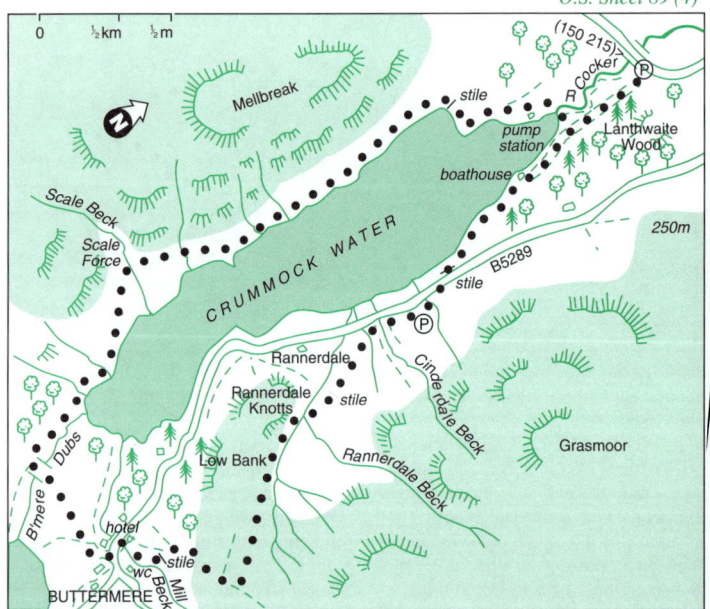

To reach the start of this route, drive west from Keswick on the A66 for Cockermouth. After two miles, turn left onto the B5292; immediately passing through Braithwaite and then crossing Whinlatter Pass into Lorton Vale. Follow the signs for Buttermere which lead onto the B5289. Follow this for two miles until the Buttermere road swings left and the minor road for Loweswater

continues straight ahead. Follow the latter for one mile and then turn left into the Lanthwaite Wood car park.

Go through the gate at the edge of the car park and follow a clear track through the woodland, parallel to the river down to the right. Various tracks and paths cut off to the left in this woodland section. Ignore these. After half a mile (1km) the track reaches the lake and continues by the waterside. Just before a boathouse is reached the path splits. Keep to the right; dropping down, past the boathouse, and then continuing on a rough path which climbs across a small wooded peninsula. Shortly beyond this there is a stile over a dyke. Cross this and continue along the clear, rough, path above the lake edge.

The path quickly enters an area of open grassland and gorse, with the public road converging with the shore from the left. Climb up at this point, cross the stile over the dyke, and continue along the clear verge on the far side of the road as far as the car park before Cinderdale Beck. At this point there is a choice. For a slightly shorter, slightly less steep route, carry straight on along the roadside and then follow the clear path over the end of Rannerdale Knotts (fine views) before dropping back down to the road and continuing to Buttermere village. The problem with this alternative is that it does necessitate walking by the side of the – often busy – public road. For a pleasant alternative, via Rannerdale, swing away from the road beyond the car park, following a faint footpath across the beck and then along a clearer track with a dyke to the right. When the dyke runs across the way, cross it at a stile and continue up the narrowing dale; crossing the beck and then climbing up beyond to join a clear track. A turn to the right will bring you back down to the road. For this route, however, turn left and continue up to the head of the dale.

The path climbs to a watershed, providing a wonderful view over Buttermere. Turn right. Almost immediately a path cuts to the right,

climbing over Low Bank. Ignore this and follow the path which continues down the lower ridge towards Buttermere. Watch for the wood by the side of the beck, down to the left, and follow one of the numerous rough paths which lead down to it. Near the top of the wood there is a stile over a dyke. Cross this and follow the path beyond down to the bridge in Buttermere.

Go through the gate at the bottom of the wood, swing left, then right at the sign for the footpath to Buttermere and Scale Force. Walk down to the left of the Fish Hotel and continue on the clear track beyond; swinging first to the left and then to the right. At the latter point, the track splits. Go right here and follow the track to the old stone bridge over Buttermere Dubs. Turn right beyond on a clear track with a wooded slope to the left.

This track is clear at first, but gradually becomes less so when it leaves the woodland and the dale of the Scale Beck opens up to the left. There are numerous paths through this section; all of them faint, all of them wet. Follow whichever of them appears most obvious, leading up the dale to the foot of the dramatic Scale Force. Cross the beck below the waterfall and take the rough, clear footpath which leads down its far side to the lakeside, then continue by the water.

Just before the end of the lake there is a large peninsula. Cross the stile over the dyke just before this and then continue along a fainter path by the waterside. Follow this past an old pump house then on beyond; up to a foot-bridge over the River Cocker, where it exits the lake. Climb up beyond this to rejoin the original track.

A short circuit by a small lake, through farmland and woodland by the water's edge and along the open hillside above. Paths generally clear.
Length: **7 miles/11km**; *Height Climbed:* **650ft/200m.**

O.S. Sheets 89 or 90 (4)

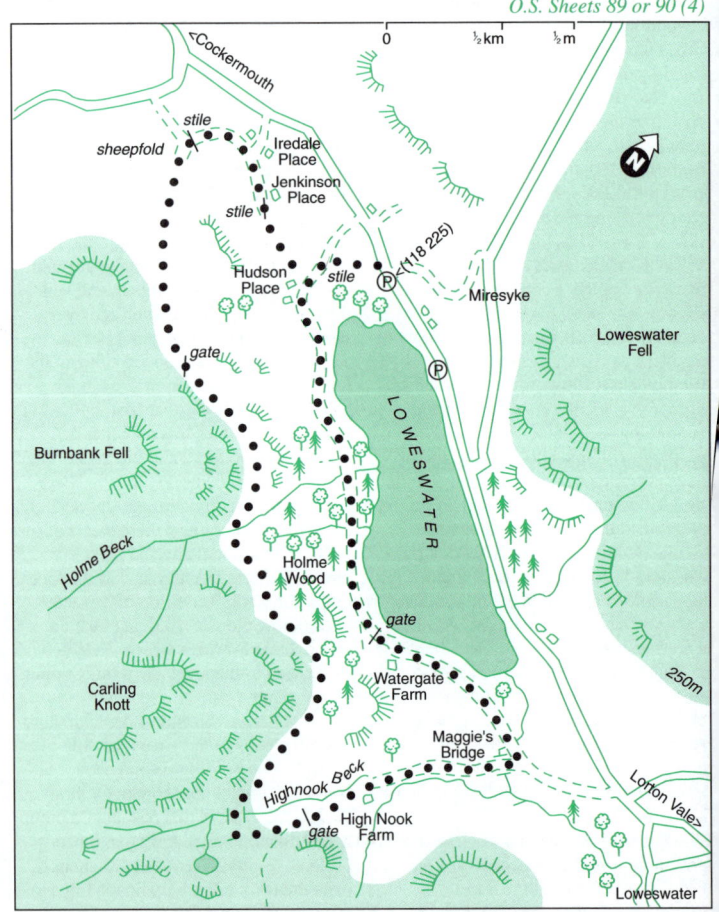

To reach the start of this route, drive west from Keswick on the A66 road for Cockermouth. After two miles, turn left onto the B5292; passing immediately through Braithwaite and then crossing Whinlatter Pass into Lorton Vale. Follow the signs for Buttermere which lead onto the B5289. Continue along this for two miles until the Buttermere road swings off to the left and the minor road for Loweswater continues straight ahead. Follow the latter for three miles to a car park, to the left of the road, just beyond the end of Loweswater.

From the far end of the car park, turn left through a gate marked by a signpost for the public footpath. Follow this path down the left-hand side of a small rill, then jink across this into a field and continue down the hill, moving away from the rill, towards a bridge of duckboards across a marshy area at the foot of the slope. Climb up the field beyond to a stile leading onto a metalled road. Turn left along this.

At Hudson Place farm there is a three-way junction: go straight ahead, following the sign for Holme Wood; passing through the farm and then turning left on a clear track leading down towards the lake. Follow the track through the woods by the lake, finally exiting the trees by a gate near the waterside, with Watergate Farm visible beyond. Turn left in front of the farm, following a clear track across a flat area of fields to the small car park at Maggie's Bridge. Turn right from the car park, over the bridge, and follow the track which leads across the fields and on up to High Nook Farm before continuing up the narrowing dale of Highnook Beck beyond.

After passing through a gate in a dyke, a clear track heads off to the left. Ignore this and continue climbing with the beck to the right. The path now becomes faint, but look ahead for a bridge over the beck. Cross this and follow the clear track beyond, climbing up and across the slope to run along the face of the hill above the conifer plantation of Holme Wood. There are fine views of the lake and the surrounding hills from this section of the route.

When the wood ends the track continues; contouring round the slope to a gate in a dyke. Go through this and turn right, continuing across an area of open grassland with the dyke to the right. Continue until a sign indicates a public footpath to Hudson's Place leading off to the right.

Cross a stile and follow the path, with a dyke to the right, down to Iredale Place. Pass to the right of this and continue on a metalled drive past Jenkinson Place. Just beyond this, cut left across a stile and continue on a grassy track leading across the field beyond to a dyke. Pass through a gap in this dyke and then continue to the right of a line of hawthorn trees. At the end of the field, ignore the field gate which opens to the left and continue along a clear track to a further gate with a stile beside it. Cross this and continue to the right of a fence. Hudson's Place is visible ahead. Just before the farm, turn left; crossing a stile and skirting round to the left of the farm to reach a stile leading onto a clear track. Turn left and retrace your steps to return to the start.

A group of signposted forest and woodland walks to the west of Keswick. Walks 1–4 (with their variations) are in the Whinlatter Forest Park and are maintained by the Forestry Commission: a leaflet providing detailed maps and information on these routes is available from the Whinlatter Visitor Centre (see map). Walk 5 is a short route through broad-leaved woodland on the slopes above Bassenthwaite Lake. O.S. Sheets 89 or 90 (4)

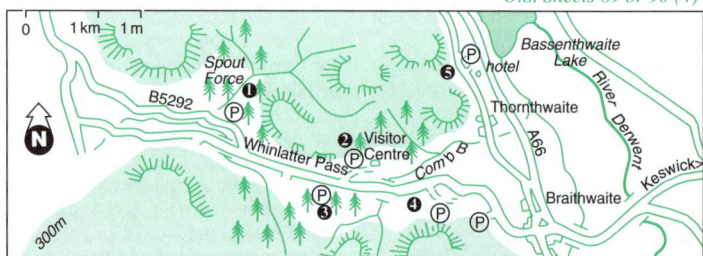

To reach Whinlatter Forest Park, drive west from the centre of Keswick on the B5289 to join the A66. Drive a further mile west on this and then turn left onto the B5292. The road goes through the little village of Braithwaite and then climbs into the hills beyond, signposted for Whinlatter Pass. The Visitor Centre is two miles along this road, with further car parks spread out along the road on either side (see map).

1 Spout Force. One route, 1½ miles (2.5km) in length, leading through conifer woodland to a fine view of a steep waterfall. Steep in places.

2 Visitor Centre. Two routes, Red and Blue, both 1¾ miles (2.75km) in length; passing through conifer plantations on the steep hillside and by the side of the little Comb Beck. Viewpoints and information boards.

3 Revelin Moss. One route, 2 miles (3km) in length, passing through conifer plantations on the lower slopes of Grisedale Pike. Comparatively flat, and providing some of the easiest walking in these forest trails.

4 Noble Knott. Four routes: Red, ¼ mile (0.3km); Blue, ½ mile (1km); Yellow, 1 mile (1.5km); White, 1¾ miles (2.75km). A selection of routes through an area of mixed woodland. Slopes fairly gentle and fine views of Bassenthwaite, Skiddaw and Keswick from the start.

5 Powter How (not part of forest park). One route, ¾ miles (1.25km) in length; a flat walk passing through mixed woodland with views over Bassenthwaite Lake. To reach the start, follow the driving instructions above, but turn right in Braithwaite. Follow this road for two miles to the Swan Hotel. Just beyond this there is a car park to the right of the road. Walk out of the back of this and follow the clear path around the base of the wooded hill beyond.

(Continued from Page 1)

made through the shore's woodland and the open hills above (*7*). To the west, a link through the village of Portinscale (*10*) leads to a moderate climb along the narrow ridge of Cat Bells with a return by the lakeside (*11*). With the aid of a good map, these various walks can be strung together to make a complete circuit of the lake.

Beyond the southern end of Derwent Water is Borrowdale. At the head of the lake the River Derwent meanders through a broad, flat flood-plane, but above Grange this narrows to a rocky, wooded valley (*13*), before opening out again around Rosthwaite. Beyond this the valley of the tributary Stonethwaite Beck (*12*) heads off to the south-east, leading up to the high hill passes into Great Langdale, while the Derwent swings south-west past the little hamlet at Seatoller (*14*) and climbs up to the passes leading to Wasdale and Eskdale, and the paths up Great Gable and Scafell Pike. Between the two dales is the craggy peak of Glaramara (*15*), from where there are spectacular views of these great hills.

At Seatoller the B5289 leaves the River Derwent and swings west to make the steep climb over Honister Pass (*16*) before dropping down to the southern end of Buttermere, with its dramatic serrated ridge – including Hay Stacks (*17*) – to the south. There are low-level paths around both Buttermere (*18*) and Crummock Water (*20*) – the larger lake to the north – as well as a short walk to Crummock Water from the hamlet of Buttermere (*19*). North of the lakes the River Cocker runs through the broadening Lorton Vale. In the low hills to the west is the little lake of Loweswater (*21*), while the B5292 cuts east over the high Whinlatter pass; dropping through extensive conifer woodland (*22*) to reach the village of Braithwaite, two miles west of Keswick. To the south-west the bare crest of Grisedale Pike (*9*) rises above Coledale.

———————————

Hallewell Publications also produce the following local titles in the same series:

    □ **Walks Grasmere, Ambleside & Windermere**
    □ **Walks Ullswater & the Eastern Lakes**

These are available from bookshops locally, or direct from the publishers (£2.20, including p+p). For a full list of other titles in this and other companion series please send an SAE to:

Hallewell Publications, Port-an-Eilean, Strathtummel, Pitlochry PH16 5RU

Walks: Keswick
& the Northern Lakes

●

26 walks:
2-10 miles (3-16km)

●

Graded for difficulty

●

Route maps and descriptions

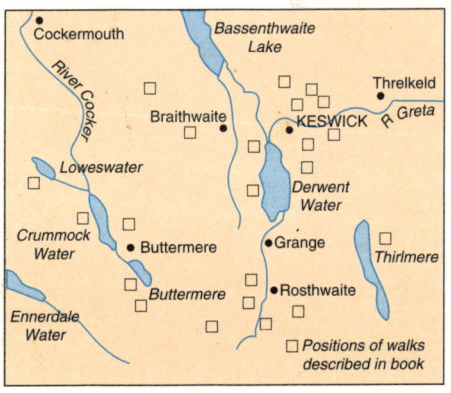

Cockermouth
Bassenthwaite Lake
Threlkeld
River Cocker
Braithwaite
KESWICK
R Greta
Loweswater
Derwent Water
Crummock Water
Buttermere
Grange
Thirlmere
Buttermere
Rosthwaite
Ennerdale Water

□ *Positions of walks described in book*

ISBN 1-872405-04-5

£1.95

9 781872 405049